This Book Belongs To

_____

Design name: _____

Dimensions: _____

Purchased kit from: _____

Price: _____

If the kit was a gift, who was it from? _____

Date started: _____

Date completed: _____

Difficulty level: ◇ Beginner ◇ Intermediate ◇ Advanced

What I did with the finished piece:

◇ Kept it   ◇ Gifted it   ◇ Sold it   ◇ Other

If gifted or sold, who was the recipient? _____

If sold, what was the price? _____

My overall rating of this product: ◇ ◇ ◇ ◇ ◇

Additional notes about this project: _____

_____

_____

_____

_____

_____

Next project planned: _____

_____

_____

Design name: _____

Dimensions: _____

Purchased kit from: _____

Price: _____

If the kit was a gift, who was it from? _____

Date started: _____

Date completed: _____

Difficulty level: ◇ Beginner   ◇ Intermediate   ◇ Advanced

What I did with the finished piece:

◇ Kept it   ◇ Gifted it   ◇ Sold it   ◇ Other

If gifted or sold, who was the recipient? _____

If sold, what was the price? _____

My overall rating of this product: ◇ ◇ ◇ ◇ ◇

Additional notes about this project: _____

_____

_____

_____

_____

_____

Next project planned: _____

_____

_____

Design name: _____

Dimensions: _____

Purchased kit from: _____

Price: _____

If the kit was a gift, who was it from? _____

Date started: _____

Date completed: _____

Difficulty level: ◇ Beginner   ◇ Intermediate   ◇ Advanced

What I did with the finished piece:

◇ Kept it   ◇ Gifted it   ◇ Sold it   ◇ Other

If gifted or sold, who was the recipient? _____

If sold, what was the price? _____

My overall rating of this product: ◇ ◇ ◇ ◇ ◇

Additional notes about this project: _____

_____

_____

_____

_____

_____

Next project planned: _____

_____

_____

Design name: _____

Dimensions: _____

Purchased kit from: _____

Price: _____

If the kit was a gift, who was it from? _____

Date started: _____

Date completed: _____

Difficulty level: ◇ Beginner   ◇ Intermediate   ◇ Advanced

What I did with the finished piece:

◇ Kept it   ◇ Gifted it   ◇ Sold it   ◇ Other

If gifted or sold, who was the recipient? _____

If sold, what was the price? _____

My overall rating of this product: ◇ ◇ ◇ ◇ ◇

Additional notes about this project: _____

_____

_____

_____

_____

_____

Next project planned: _____

_____

_____

Design name: _____

Dimensions: _____

Purchased kit from: _____

Price: _____

If the kit was a gift, who was it from? _____

Date started: _____

Date completed: _____

Difficulty level: ◇ Beginner ◇ Intermediate ◇ Advanced

What I did with the finished piece:

◇ Kept it ◇ Gifted it ◇ Sold it ◇ Other

If gifted or sold, who was the recipient? _____

If sold, what was the price? _____

My overall rating of this product: ◇ ◇ ◇ ◇ ◇

Additional notes about this project: _____

_____

_____

_____

_____

_____

Next project planned: _____

_____

_____

Design name: _____

Dimensions: _____

Purchased kit from: _____

Price: _____

If the kit was a gift, who was it from? _____

Date started: _____

Date completed: _____

Difficulty level: ◇ Beginner   ◇ Intermediate   ◇ Advanced

What I did with the finished piece:

◇ Kept it   ◇ Gifted it   ◇ Sold it   ◇ Other

If gifted or sold, who was the recipient? _____

If sold, what was the price? _____

My overall rating of this product: ◇ ◇ ◇ ◇ ◇

Additional notes about this project: _____

_____

_____

_____

_____

_____

Next project planned: _____

_____

_____

Design name: _____

Dimensions: _____

Purchased kit from: _____

Price: _____

If the kit was a gift, who was it from? _____

Date started: _____

Date completed: _____

Difficulty level: ◇ Beginner   ◇ Intermediate   ◇ Advanced

What I did with the finished piece:

◇ Kept it   ◇ Gifted it   ◇ Sold it   ◇ Other

If gifted or sold, who was the recipient? _____

If sold, what was the price? _____

My overall rating of this product: ◇ ◇ ◇ ◇ ◇

Additional notes about this project: _____

_____

_____

_____

_____

_____

Next project planned: _____

_____

_____

Design name: _____

Dimensions: _____

Purchased kit from: _____

Price: _____

If the kit was a gift, who was it from? _____

Date started: _____

Date completed: _____

Difficulty level: ◇ Beginner   ◇ Intermediate   ◇ Advanced

What I did with the finished piece:

◇ Kept it   ◇ Gifted it   ◇ Sold it   ◇ Other

If gifted or sold, who was the recipient? _____

If sold, what was the price? _____

My overall rating of this product: ◇ ◇ ◇ ◇ ◇

Additional notes about this project: _____

_____

_____

_____

_____

_____

Next project planned: _____

_____

_____

Design name: _____

Dimensions: _____

Purchased kit from: _____

Price: _____

If the kit was a gift, who was it from? _____

Date started: _____

Date completed: _____

Difficulty level: ◇ Beginner ◇ Intermediate ◇ Advanced

What I did with the finished piece:

◇ Kept it ◇ Gifted it ◇ Sold it ◇ Other

If gifted or sold, who was the recipient? _____

If sold, what was the price? _____

My overall rating of this product: ◇ ◇ ◇ ◇ ◇

Additional notes about this project: _____

_____

_____

_____

_____

_____

Next project planned: _____

_____

_____

Design name: _____

Dimensions: _____

Purchased kit from: _____

Price: _____

If the kit was a gift, who was it from? _____

Date started: _____

Date completed: _____

Difficulty level: ◇ Beginner   ◇ Intermediate   ◇ Advanced

What I did with the finished piece:

◇ Kept it   ◇ Gifted it   ◇ Sold it   ◇ Other

If gifted or sold, who was the recipient? _____

If sold, what was the price? _____

My overall rating of this product: ◇ ◇ ◇ ◇ ◇

Additional notes about this project: _____

_____

_____

_____

_____

_____

Next project planned: _____

_____

_____

Design name: _____

Dimensions: _____

Purchased kit from: _____

Price: _____

If the kit was a gift, who was it from? _____

Date started: _____

Date completed: _____

Difficulty level: ◇ Beginner   ◇ Intermediate   ◇ Advanced

What I did with the finished piece:

◇ Kept it   ◇ Gifted it   ◇ Sold it   ◇ Other

If gifted or sold, who was the recipient? _____

If sold, what was the price? _____

My overall rating of this product: ◇ ◇ ◇ ◇ ◇

Additional notes about this project: _____

_____

_____

_____

_____

_____

Next project planned: _____

_____

_____

Design name: _____

Dimensions: _____

Purchased kit from: _____

Price: _____

If the kit was a gift, who was it from? _____

Date started: _____

Date completed: _____

Difficulty level: ◇ Beginner   ◇ Intermediate   ◇ Advanced

What I did with the finished piece:

◇ Kept it   ◇ Gifted it   ◇ Sold it   ◇ Other

If gifted or sold, who was the recipient? _____

If sold, what was the price? _____

My overall rating of this product: ◇ ◇ ◇ ◇ ◇

Additional notes about this project: _____

_____

_____

_____

_____

_____

Next project planned: _____

_____

_____

Design name: _____

Dimensions: _____

Purchased kit from: _____

Price: _____

If the kit was a gift, who was it from? _____

Date started: _____

Date completed: _____

Difficulty level: ◇ Beginner ◇ Intermediate ◇ Advanced

What I did with the finished piece:

◇ Kept it ◇ Gifted it ◇ Sold it ◇ Other

If gifted or sold, who was the recipient? _____

If sold, what was the price? _____

My overall rating of this product: ◇ ◇ ◇ ◇ ◇

Additional notes about this project: _____

_____

_____

_____

_____

_____

Next project planned: _____

_____

_____

Design name: _____

Dimensions: _____

Purchased kit from: _____

Price: _____

If the kit was a gift, who was it from? _____

Date started: _____

Date completed: _____

Difficulty level: ◇ Beginner ◇ Intermediate ◇ Advanced

What I did with the finished piece:

◇ Kept it ◇ Gifted it ◇ Sold it ◇ Other

If gifted or sold, who was the recipient? _____

If sold, what was the price? _____

My overall rating of this product: ◇ ◇ ◇ ◇ ◇

Additional notes about this project: _____

_____

_____

_____

_____

_____

Next project planned: _____

_____

_____

Design name: _____

Dimensions: _____

Purchased kit from: _____

Price: _____

If the kit was a gift, who was it from? _____

Date started: _____

Date completed: _____

Difficulty level: ◇ Beginner ◇ Intermediate ◇ Advanced

What I did with the finished piece:

◇ Kept it ◇ Gifted it ◇ Sold it ◇ Other

If gifted or sold, who was the recipient? _____

If sold, what was the price? _____

My overall rating of this product: ◇ ◇ ◇ ◇ ◇

Additional notes about this project: _____

_____

_____

_____

_____

_____

Next project planned: _____

_____

_____

Design name: _____

Dimensions: _____

Purchased kit from: _____

Price: _____

If the kit was a gift, who was it from? _____

Date started: _____

Date completed: _____

Difficulty level: ◇ Beginner ◇ Intermediate ◇ Advanced

What I did with the finished piece:

◇ Kept it ◇ Gifted it ◇ Sold it ◇ Other

If gifted or sold, who was the recipient? _____

If sold, what was the price? _____

My overall rating of this product: ◇ ◇ ◇ ◇ ◇

Additional notes about this project: _____

_____

_____

_____

_____

_____

Next project planned: _____

_____

_____

Design name: _____

Dimensions: _____

Purchased kit from: _____

Price: _____

If the kit was a gift, who was it from? _____

Date started: _____

Date completed: _____

Difficulty level: ◇ Beginner ◇ Intermediate ◇ Advanced

What I did with the finished piece:

◇ Kept it ◇ Gifted it ◇ Sold it ◇ Other

If gifted or sold, who was the recipient? _____

If sold, what was the price? _____

My overall rating of this product: ◇ ◇ ◇ ◇ ◇

Additional notes about this project: _____

_____

_____

_____

_____

_____

Next project planned: _____

_____

_____

Design name: _____

Dimensions: _____

Purchased kit from: _____

Price: _____

If the kit was a gift, who was it from? _____

Date started: _____

Date completed: _____

Difficulty level: ◇ Beginner   ◇ Intermediate   ◇ Advanced

What I did with the finished piece:

◇ Kept it   ◇ Gifted it   ◇ Sold it   ◇ Other

If gifted or sold, who was the recipient? _____

If sold, what was the price? _____

My overall rating of this product: ◇ ◇ ◇ ◇ ◇

Additional notes about this project: _____

_____

_____

_____

_____

_____

Next project planned: _____

_____

_____

Design name: _____

Dimensions: _____

Purchased kit from: _____

Price: _____

If the kit was a gift, who was it from? _____

Date started: _____

Date completed: _____

Difficulty level: ◇ Beginner   ◇ Intermediate   ◇ Advanced

What I did with the finished piece:

◇ Kept it   ◇ Gifted it   ◇ Sold it   ◇ Other

If gifted or sold, who was the recipient? _____

If sold, what was the price? _____

My overall rating of this product: ◇ ◇ ◇ ◇ ◇

Additional notes about this project: _____

_____

_____

_____

_____

_____

Next project planned: _____

_____

_____

Design name: _____

Dimensions: _____

Purchased kit from: _____

Price: _____

If the kit was a gift, who was it from? _____

Date started: _____

Date completed: _____

Difficulty level: ◇ Beginner   ◇ Intermediate   ◇ Advanced

What I did with the finished piece:

◇ Kept it   ◇ Gifted it   ◇ Sold it   ◇ Other

If gifted or sold, who was the recipient? _____

If sold, what was the price? _____

My overall rating of this product: ◇ ◇ ◇ ◇ ◇

Additional notes about this project: _____

_____

_____

_____

_____

_____

Next project planned: _____

_____

_____

Design name: _____

Dimensions: _____

Purchased kit from: _____

Price: _____

If the kit was a gift, who was it from? _____

Date started: _____

Date completed: _____

Difficulty level: ◇ Beginner ◇ Intermediate ◇ Advanced

What I did with the finished piece:

◇ Kept it ◇ Gifted it ◇ Sold it ◇ Other

If gifted or sold, who was the recipient? _____

If sold, what was the price? _____

My overall rating of this product: ◇ ◇ ◇ ◇ ◇

Additional notes about this project: _____

_____

_____

_____

_____

_____

Next project planned: _____

_____

_____

Design name: _____

Dimensions: _____

Purchased kit from: _____

Price: _____

If the kit was a gift, who was it from? _____

Date started: _____

Date completed: _____

Difficulty level: ◇ Beginner ◇ Intermediate ◇ Advanced

What I did with the finished piece:

◇ Kept it ◇ Gifted it ◇ Sold it ◇ Other

If gifted or sold, who was the recipient? _____

If sold, what was the price? _____

My overall rating of this product: ◇ ◇ ◇ ◇ ◇

Additional notes about this project: _____

_____

_____

_____

_____

_____

Next project planned: _____

_____

_____

Design name: _____

Dimensions: _____

Purchased kit from: _____

Price: _____

If the kit was a gift, who was it from? _____

Date started: _____

Date completed: _____

Difficulty level: ◇ Beginner   ◇ Intermediate   ◇ Advanced

What I did with the finished piece:

◇ Kept it   ◇ Gifted it   ◇ Sold it   ◇ Other

If gifted or sold, who was the recipient? _____

If sold, what was the price? _____

My overall rating of this product: ◇ ◇ ◇ ◇ ◇

Additional notes about this project: _____

_____

_____

_____

_____

_____

Next project planned: _____

_____

_____

Design name: _____

Dimensions: _____

Purchased kit from: _____

Price: _____

If the kit was a gift, who was it from? _____

Date started: _____

Date completed: _____

Difficulty level: ◇ Beginner   ◇ Intermediate   ◇ Advanced

What I did with the finished piece:

◇ Kept it   ◇ Gifted it   ◇ Sold it   ◇ Other

If gifted or sold, who was the recipient? _____

If sold, what was the price? _____

My overall rating of this product: ◇ ◇ ◇ ◇ ◇

Additional notes about this project: _____

_____

_____

_____

_____

_____

Next project planned: _____

_____

_____

Design name: _____

Dimensions: _____

Purchased kit from: _____

Price: _____

If the kit was a gift, who was it from? _____

Date started: _____

Date completed: _____

Difficulty level: ◇ Beginner ◇ Intermediate ◇ Advanced

What I did with the finished piece:

◇ Kept it ◇ Gifted it ◇ Sold it ◇ Other

If gifted or sold, who was the recipient? _____

If sold, what was the price? _____

My overall rating of this product: ◇ ◇ ◇ ◇ ◇

Additional notes about this project: _____

_____

_____

_____

_____

_____

Next project planned: _____

_____

_____

Design name: _____

Dimensions: _____

Purchased kit from: _____

Price: _____

If the kit was a gift, who was it from? _____

Date started: _____

Date completed: _____

Difficulty level: ◇ Beginner ◇ Intermediate ◇ Advanced

What I did with the finished piece:

◇ Kept it ◇ Gifted it ◇ Sold it ◇ Other

If gifted or sold, who was the recipient? _____

If sold, what was the price? _____

My overall rating of this product: ◇ ◇ ◇ ◇ ◇

Additional notes about this project: _____

_____

_____

_____

_____

_____

Next project planned: _____

_____

_____

Design name: _____

Dimensions: _____

Purchased kit from: _____

Price: _____

If the kit was a gift, who was it from? _____

Date started: _____

Date completed: _____

Difficulty level: ◇ Beginner   ◇ Intermediate   ◇ Advanced

What I did with the finished piece:

◇ Kept it   ◇ Gifted it   ◇ Sold it   ◇ Other

If gifted or sold, who was the recipient? _____

If sold, what was the price? _____

My overall rating of this product: ◇ ◇ ◇ ◇ ◇

Additional notes about this project: _____

_____

_____

_____

_____

_____

Next project planned: _____

_____

_____

Design name: _____

Dimensions: _____

Purchased kit from: _____

Price: _____

If the kit was a gift, who was it from? _____

Date started: _____

Date completed: _____

Difficulty level: ◇ Beginner ◇ Intermediate ◇ Advanced

What I did with the finished piece:

◇ Kept it ◇ Gifted it ◇ Sold it ◇ Other

If gifted or sold, who was the recipient? _____

If sold, what was the price? _____

My overall rating of this product: ◇ ◇ ◇ ◇ ◇

Additional notes about this project: _____

_____

_____

_____

_____

_____

Next project planned: _____

_____

_____

Design name: _____

Dimensions: _____

Purchased kit from: _____

Price: _____

If the kit was a gift, who was it from? _____

Date started: _____

Date completed: _____

Difficulty level: ◇ Beginner   ◇ Intermediate   ◇ Advanced

What I did with the finished piece:

◇ Kept it   ◇ Gifted it   ◇ Sold it   ◇ Other

If gifted or sold, who was the recipient? _____

If sold, what was the price? _____

My overall rating of this product: ◇ ◇ ◇ ◇ ◇

Additional notes about this project: _____

_____

_____

_____

_____

_____

Next project planned: _____

_____

_____

Design name: _____

Dimensions: _____

Purchased kit from: _____

Price: _____

If the kit was a gift, who was it from? _____

Date started: _____

Date completed: _____

Difficulty level: ◇ Beginner ◇ Intermediate ◇ Advanced

What I did with the finished piece:

◇ Kept it ◇ Gifted it ◇ Sold it ◇ Other

If gifted or sold, who was the recipient? _____

If sold, what was the price? _____

My overall rating of this product: ◇ ◇ ◇ ◇ ◇

Additional notes about this project: _____

_____

_____

_____

_____

_____

Next project planned: _____

_____

_____

Design name: _____

Dimensions: _____

Purchased kit from: _____

Price: _____

If the kit was a gift, who was it from? _____

Date started: _____

Date completed: _____

Difficulty level: ◇ Beginner   ◇ Intermediate   ◇ Advanced

What I did with the finished piece:

◇ Kept it   ◇ Gifted it   ◇ Sold it   ◇ Other

If gifted or sold, who was the recipient? _____

If sold, what was the price? _____

My overall rating of this product: ◇ ◇ ◇ ◇ ◇

Additional notes about this project: _____

_____

_____

_____

_____

_____

Next project planned: _____

_____

_____

Design name: _____

Dimensions: _____

Purchased kit from: _____

Price: _____

If the kit was a gift, who was it from? _____

Date started: _____

Date completed: _____

Difficulty level: ◇ Beginner ◇ Intermediate ◇ Advanced

What I did with the finished piece:

◇ Kept it   ◇ Gifted it   ◇ Sold it   ◇ Other

If gifted or sold, who was the recipient? _____

If sold, what was the price? _____

My overall rating of this product: ◇ ◇ ◇ ◇ ◇

Additional notes about this project: _____

_____

_____

_____

_____

_____

Next project planned: _____

_____

_____

Design name: _____

Dimensions: _____

Purchased kit from: _____

Price: _____

If the kit was a gift, who was it from? _____

Date started: _____

Date completed: _____

Difficulty level: ◇ Beginner ◇ Intermediate ◇ Advanced

What I did with the finished piece:

◇ Kept it ◇ Gifted it ◇ Sold it ◇ Other

If gifted or sold, who was the recipient? _____

If sold, what was the price? _____

My overall rating of this product: ◇ ◇ ◇ ◇ ◇

Additional notes about this project: _____

_____

_____

_____

_____

_____

Next project planned: _____

_____

_____

Design name: _____

Dimensions: _____

Purchased kit from: _____

Price: _____

If the kit was a gift, who was it from? _____

Date started: _____

Date completed: _____

Difficulty level: ◇ Beginner   ◇ Intermediate   ◇ Advanced

What I did with the finished piece:

◇ Kept it   ◇ Gifted it   ◇ Sold it   ◇ Other

If gifted or sold, who was the recipient? _____

If sold, what was the price? _____

My overall rating of this product: ◇ ◇ ◇ ◇ ◇

Additional notes about this project: _____

_____

_____

_____

_____

_____

Next project planned: _____

_____

_____

Design name: _____

Dimensions: _____

Purchased kit from: _____

Price: _____

If the kit was a gift, who was it from? _____

Date started: _____

Date completed: _____

Difficulty level: ◇ Beginner   ◇ Intermediate   ◇ Advanced

What I did with the finished piece:

◇ Kept it   ◇ Gifted it   ◇ Sold it   ◇ Other

If gifted or sold, who was the recipient? _____

If sold, what was the price? _____

My overall rating of this product: ◇ ◇ ◇ ◇ ◇

Additional notes about this project: _____

_____

_____

_____

_____

_____

Next project planned: _____

_____

_____

Design name: _____

Dimensions: _____

Purchased kit from: _____

Price: _____

If the kit was a gift, who was it from? _____

Date started: _____

Date completed: _____

Difficulty level: ◇ Beginner   ◇ Intermediate   ◇ Advanced

What I did with the finished piece:

◇ Kept it   ◇ Gifted it   ◇ Sold it   ◇ Other

If gifted or sold, who was the recipient? _____

If sold, what was the price? _____

My overall rating of this product: ◇ ◇ ◇ ◇ ◇

Additional notes about this project: _____

_____

_____

_____

_____

_____

Next project planned: _____

_____

_____

Design name: _____

Dimensions: _____

Purchased kit from: _____

Price: _____

If the kit was a gift, who was it from? _____

Date started: _____

Date completed: _____

Difficulty level: ◇ Beginner   ◇ Intermediate   ◇ Advanced

What I did with the finished piece:

◇ Kept it   ◇ Gifted it   ◇ Sold it   ◇ Other

If gifted or sold, who was the recipient? _____

If sold, what was the price? _____

My overall rating of this product: ◇ ◇ ◇ ◇ ◇

Additional notes about this project: _____

_____

_____

_____

_____

_____

Next project planned: _____

_____

_____

Design name: _____

Dimensions: _____

Purchased kit from: _____

Price: _____

If the kit was a gift, who was it from? _____

Date started: _____

Date completed: _____

Difficulty level: ◇ Beginner   ◇ Intermediate   ◇ Advanced

What I did with the finished piece:

◇ Kept it   ◇ Gifted it   ◇ Sold it   ◇ Other

If gifted or sold, who was the recipient? _____

If sold, what was the price? _____

My overall rating of this product: ◇ ◇ ◇ ◇ ◇

Additional notes about this project: _____

_____

_____

_____

_____

_____

Next project planned: _____

_____

_____

Design name: _____

Dimensions: _____

Purchased kit from: _____

Price: _____

If the kit was a gift, who was it from? _____

Date started: _____

Date completed: _____

Difficulty level: ◇ Beginner   ◇ Intermediate   ◇ Advanced

What I did with the finished piece:

◇ Kept it   ◇ Gifted it   ◇ Sold it   ◇ Other

If gifted or sold, who was the recipient? _____

If sold, what was the price? _____

My overall rating of this product: ◇ ◇ ◇ ◇ ◇

Additional notes about this project: _____

_____

_____

_____

_____

_____

Next project planned: _____

_____

_____

Design name: _____

Dimensions: _____

Purchased kit from: _____

Price: _____

If the kit was a gift, who was it from? _____

Date started: _____

Date completed: _____

Difficulty level: ◇ Beginner   ◇ Intermediate   ◇ Advanced

What I did with the finished piece:

◇ Kept it   ◇ Gifted it   ◇ Sold it   ◇ Other

If gifted or sold, who was the recipient? _____

If sold, what was the price? _____

My overall rating of this product: ◇ ◇ ◇ ◇ ◇

Additional notes about this project: _____

_____

_____

_____

_____

_____

Next project planned: _____

_____

_____

Design name: _____

Dimensions: _____

Purchased kit from: _____

Price: _____

If the kit was a gift, who was it from? _____

Date started: _____

Date completed: _____

Difficulty level: ◇ Beginner   ◇ Intermediate   ◇ Advanced

What I did with the finished piece:

◇ Kept it   ◇ Gifted it   ◇ Sold it   ◇ Other

If gifted or sold, who was the recipient? _____

If sold, what was the price? _____

My overall rating of this product: ◇ ◇ ◇ ◇ ◇

Additional notes about this project: _____

_____

_____

_____

_____

_____

Next project planned: _____

_____

_____

Design name: _____

Dimensions: _____

Purchased kit from: _____

Price: _____

If the kit was a gift, who was it from? _____

Date started: _____

Date completed: _____

Difficulty level: ◇ Beginner   ◇ Intermediate   ◇ Advanced

What I did with the finished piece:

◇ Kept it   ◇ Gifted it   ◇ Sold it   ◇ Other

If gifted or sold, who was the recipient? _____

If sold, what was the price? _____

My overall rating of this product: ◇ ◇ ◇ ◇ ◇

Additional notes about this project: _____

_____

_____

_____

_____

_____

Next project planned: _____

_____

_____

Design name: _____

Dimensions: _____

Purchased kit from: _____

Price: _____

If the kit was a gift, who was it from? _____

Date started: _____

Date completed: _____

Difficulty level: ◇ Beginner ◇ Intermediate ◇ Advanced

What I did with the finished piece:

◇ Kept it   ◇ Gifted it   ◇ Sold it   ◇ Other

If gifted or sold, who was the recipient? _____

If sold, what was the price? _____

My overall rating of this product: ◇ ◇ ◇ ◇ ◇

Additional notes about this project: _____

_____

_____

_____

_____

_____

Next project planned: _____

_____

_____

Design name: _____

Dimensions: _____

Purchased kit from: _____

Price: _____

If the kit was a gift, who was it from? _____

Date started: _____

Date completed: _____

Difficulty level: ◇ Beginner   ◇ Intermediate   ◇ Advanced

What I did with the finished piece:

◇ Kept it   ◇ Gifted it   ◇ Sold it   ◇ Other

If gifted or sold, who was the recipient? _____

If sold, what was the price? _____

My overall rating of this product: ◇ ◇ ◇ ◇ ◇

Additional notes about this project: _____

_____

_____

_____

_____

_____

Next project planned: _____

_____

_____

Design name: _____

Dimensions: _____

Purchased kit from: _____

Price: _____

If the kit was a gift, who was it from? _____

Date started: _____

Date completed: _____

Difficulty level: ◇ Beginner ◇ Intermediate ◇ Advanced

What I did with the finished piece:

◇ Kept it ◇ Gifted it ◇ Sold it ◇ Other

If gifted or sold, who was the recipient? _____

If sold, what was the price? _____

My overall rating of this product: ◇ ◇ ◇ ◇ ◇

Additional notes about this project: _____

_____

_____

_____

_____

_____

Next project planned: _____

_____

_____

Design name: _____

Dimensions: _____

Purchased kit from: _____

Price: _____

If the kit was a gift, who was it from? _____

Date started: _____

Date completed: _____

Difficulty level: ◇ Beginner   ◇ Intermediate   ◇ Advanced

What I did with the finished piece:

◇ Kept it   ◇ Gifted it   ◇ Sold it   ◇ Other

If gifted or sold, who was the recipient? _____

If sold, what was the price? _____

My overall rating of this product: ◇ ◇ ◇ ◇ ◇

Additional notes about this project: _____

_____

_____

_____

_____

_____

Next project planned: _____

_____

_____

Design name: _____

Dimensions: _____

Purchased kit from: _____

Price: _____

If the kit was a gift, who was it from? _____

Date started: _____

Date completed: _____

Difficulty level: ◇ Beginner   ◇ Intermediate   ◇ Advanced

What I did with the finished piece:

◇ Kept it   ◇ Gifted it   ◇ Sold it   ◇ Other

If gifted or sold, who was the recipient? _____

If sold, what was the price? _____

My overall rating of this product: ◇ ◇ ◇ ◇ ◇

Additional notes about this project: _____

_____

_____

_____

_____

_____

Next project planned: _____

_____

_____

Design name: _____

Dimensions: _____

Purchased kit from: _____

Price: _____

If the kit was a gift, who was it from? _____

Date started: _____

Date completed: _____

Difficulty level: ◇ Beginner ◇ Intermediate ◇ Advanced

What I did with the finished piece:

◇ Kept it ◇ Gifted it ◇ Sold it ◇ Other

If gifted or sold, who was the recipient? _____

If sold, what was the price? _____

My overall rating of this product: ◇ ◇ ◇ ◇ ◇

Additional notes about this project: _____

_____

_____

_____

_____

_____

Next project planned: _____

_____

_____

Design name: _____

Dimensions: _____

Purchased kit from: _____

Price: _____

If the kit was a gift, who was it from? _____

Date started: _____

Date completed: _____

Difficulty level: ◇ Beginner   ◇ Intermediate   ◇ Advanced

What I did with the finished piece:

◇ Kept it   ◇ Gifted it   ◇ Sold it   ◇ Other

If gifted or sold, who was the recipient? _____

If sold, what was the price? _____

My overall rating of this product: ◇ ◇ ◇ ◇ ◇

Additional notes about this project: _____

_____

_____

_____

_____

_____

Next project planned: _____

_____

_____

Design name: _____

Dimensions: _____

Purchased kit from: _____

Price: _____

If the kit was a gift, who was it from? _____

Date started: _____

Date completed: _____

Difficulty level: ◇ Beginner   ◇ Intermediate   ◇ Advanced

What I did with the finished piece:

◇ Kept it   ◇ Gifted it   ◇ Sold it   ◇ Other

If gifted or sold, who was the recipient? _____

If sold, what was the price? _____

My overall rating of this product: ◇ ◇ ◇ ◇ ◇

Additional notes about this project: _____

_____

_____

_____

_____

_____

Next project planned: _____

_____

_____

Design name: _____

Dimensions: _____

Purchased kit from: _____

Price: _____

If the kit was a gift, who was it from? _____

Date started: _____

Date completed: _____

Difficulty level: ◇ Beginner ◇ Intermediate ◇ Advanced

What I did with the finished piece:

◇ Kept it ◇ Gifted it ◇ Sold it ◇ Other

If gifted or sold, who was the recipient? _____

If sold, what was the price? _____

My overall rating of this product: ◇ ◇ ◇ ◇ ◇

Additional notes about this project: _____

_____

_____

_____

_____

_____

Next project planned: _____

_____

_____

Design name: _____

Dimensions: _____

Purchased kit from: _____

Price: _____

If the kit was a gift, who was it from? _____

Date started: _____

Date completed: _____

Difficulty level: ◇ Beginner   ◇ Intermediate   ◇ Advanced

What I did with the finished piece:

◇ Kept it   ◇ Gifted it   ◇ Sold it   ◇ Other

If gifted or sold, who was the recipient? _____

If sold, what was the price? _____

My overall rating of this product: ◇ ◇ ◇ ◇ ◇

Additional notes about this project: _____

_____

_____

_____

_____

_____

Next project planned: _____

_____

_____

Design name: _____

Dimensions: _____

Purchased kit from: _____

Price: _____

If the kit was a gift, who was it from? _____

Date started: _____

Date completed: _____

Difficulty level: ◇ Beginner   ◇ Intermediate   ◇ Advanced

What I did with the finished piece:

◇ Kept it   ◇ Gifted it   ◇ Sold it   ◇ Other

If gifted or sold, who was the recipient? _____

If sold, what was the price? _____

My overall rating of this product: ◇ ◇ ◇ ◇ ◇

Additional notes about this project: _____

_____

_____

_____

_____

Next project planned: _____

_____

_____

Design name: _____

Dimensions: _____

Purchased kit from: _____

Price: _____

If the kit was a gift, who was it from? _____

Date started: _____

Date completed: _____

Difficulty level: ◇ Beginner ◇ Intermediate ◇ Advanced

What I did with the finished piece:

◇ Kept it ◇ Gifted it ◇ Sold it ◇ Other

If gifted or sold, who was the recipient? _____

If sold, what was the price? _____

My overall rating of this product: ◇ ◇ ◇ ◇ ◇

Additional notes about this project: _____

_____

_____

_____

_____

_____

Next project planned: _____

_____

_____

Design name: _____

Dimensions: _____

Purchased kit from: _____

Price: _____

If the kit was a gift, who was it from? _____

Date started: _____

Date completed: _____

Difficulty level: ◇ Beginner   ◇ Intermediate   ◇ Advanced

What I did with the finished piece:

◇ Kept it   ◇ Gifted it   ◇ Sold it   ◇ Other

If gifted or sold, who was the recipient? _____

If sold, what was the price? _____

My overall rating of this product: ◇ ◇ ◇ ◇ ◇

Additional notes about this project: _____

_____

_____

_____

_____

_____

Next project planned: _____

_____

_____

Design name: _____

Dimensions: _____

Purchased kit from: _____

Price: _____

If the kit was a gift, who was it from? _____

Date started: _____

Date completed: _____

Difficulty level: ◇ Beginner   ◇ Intermediate   ◇ Advanced

What I did with the finished piece:

◇ Kept it   ◇ Gifted it   ◇ Sold it   ◇ Other

If gifted or sold, who was the recipient? _____

If sold, what was the price? _____

My overall rating of this product: ◇ ◇ ◇ ◇ ◇

Additional notes about this project: _____

_____

_____

_____

_____

_____

Next project planned: _____

_____

_____

Design name: _____

Dimensions: _____

Purchased kit from: _____

Price: _____

If the kit was a gift, who was it from? _____

Date started: _____

Date completed: _____

Difficulty level: ◇ Beginner ◇ Intermediate ◇ Advanced

What I did with the finished piece:

◇ Kept it ◇ Gifted it ◇ Sold it ◇ Other

If gifted or sold, who was the recipient? _____

If sold, what was the price? _____

My overall rating of this product: ◇ ◇ ◇ ◇ ◇

Additional notes about this project: _____

_____

_____

_____

_____

_____

Next project planned: _____

_____

_____

Design name: _____

Dimensions: _____

Purchased kit from: _____

Price: _____

If the kit was a gift, who was it from? _____

Date started: _____

Date completed: _____

Difficulty level: ◇ Beginner   ◇ Intermediate   ◇ Advanced

What I did with the finished piece:

◇ Kept it   ◇ Gifted it   ◇ Sold it   ◇ Other

If gifted or sold, who was the recipient? _____

If sold, what was the price? _____

My overall rating of this product: ◇ ◇ ◇ ◇ ◇

Additional notes about this project: _____

_____

_____

_____

_____

_____

Next project planned: _____

_____

_____

Design name: _____

Dimensions: _____

Purchased kit from: _____

Price: _____

If the kit was a gift, who was it from? _____

Date started: _____

Date completed: _____

Difficulty level: ◇ Beginner   ◇ Intermediate   ◇ Advanced

What I did with the finished piece:

◇ Kept it   ◇ Gifted it   ◇ Sold it   ◇ Other

If gifted or sold, who was the recipient? _____

If sold, what was the price? _____

My overall rating of this product: ◇ ◇ ◇ ◇ ◇

Additional notes about this project: _____

_____

_____

_____

_____

_____

Next project planned: _____

_____

_____

Design name: _____

Dimensions: _____

Purchased kit from: _____

Price: _____

If the kit was a gift, who was it from? _____

Date started: _____

Date completed: _____

Difficulty level: ◇ Beginner   ◇ Intermediate   ◇ Advanced

What I did with the finished piece:

◇ Kept it   ◇ Gifted it   ◇ Sold it   ◇ Other

If gifted or sold, who was the recipient? _____

If sold, what was the price? _____

My overall rating of this product: ◇ ◇ ◇ ◇ ◇

Additional notes about this project: _____

_____

_____

_____

_____

_____

Next project planned: _____

_____

_____

Design name: _____

Dimensions: _____

Purchased kit from: _____

Price: _____

If the kit was a gift, who was it from? _____

Date started: _____

Date completed: _____

Difficulty level: ◇ Beginner   ◇ Intermediate   ◇ Advanced

What I did with the finished piece:

◇ Kept it   ◇ Gifted it   ◇ Sold it   ◇ Other

If gifted or sold, who was the recipient? _____

If sold, what was the price? _____

My overall rating of this product: ◇ ◇ ◇ ◇ ◇

Additional notes about this project: _____

_____

_____

_____

_____

_____

Next project planned: _____

_____

_____

Design name: _____

Dimensions: _____

Purchased kit from: _____

Price: _____

If the kit was a gift, who was it from? _____

Date started: _____

Date completed: _____

Difficulty level: ◇ Beginner   ◇ Intermediate   ◇ Advanced

What I did with the finished piece:

◇ Kept it   ◇ Gifted it   ◇ Sold it   ◇ Other

If gifted or sold, who was the recipient? _____

If sold, what was the price? _____

My overall rating of this product: ◇ ◇ ◇ ◇ ◇

Additional notes about this project: _____

_____

_____

_____

_____

_____

Next project planned: _____

_____

_____

Design name: _____

Dimensions: _____

Purchased kit from: _____

Price: _____

If the kit was a gift, who was it from? _____

Date started: _____

Date completed: _____

Difficulty level: ◇ Beginner   ◇ Intermediate   ◇ Advanced

What I did with the finished piece:

◇ Kept it   ◇ Gifted it   ◇ Sold it   ◇ Other

If gifted or sold, who was the recipient? _____

If sold, what was the price? _____

My overall rating of this product: ◇ ◇ ◇ ◇ ◇

Additional notes about this project: _____

_____

_____

_____

_____

_____

Next project planned: _____

_____

_____

Design name: _____

Dimensions: _____

Purchased kit from: _____

Price: _____

If the kit was a gift, who was it from? _____

Date started: _____

Date completed: _____

Difficulty level: ◇ Beginner   ◇ Intermediate   ◇ Advanced

What I did with the finished piece:

◇ Kept it   ◇ Gifted it   ◇ Sold it   ◇ Other

If gifted or sold, who was the recipient? _____

If sold, what was the price? _____

My overall rating of this product: ◇ ◇ ◇ ◇ ◇

Additional notes about this project: _____

_____

_____

_____

_____

_____

Next project planned: _____

_____

_____

Design name: _____

Dimensions: _____

Purchased kit from: _____

Price: _____

If the kit was a gift, who was it from? _____

Date started: _____

Date completed: _____

Difficulty level: ◇ Beginner ◇ Intermediate ◇ Advanced

What I did with the finished piece:

◇ Kept it ◇ Gifted it ◇ Sold it ◇ Other

If gifted or sold, who was the recipient? _____

If sold, what was the price? _____

My overall rating of this product: ◇ ◇ ◇ ◇ ◇

Additional notes about this project: _____

_____

_____

_____

_____

_____

Next project planned: _____

_____

_____

Design name: _____

Dimensions: _____

Purchased kit from: _____

Price: _____

If the kit was a gift, who was it from? _____

Date started: _____

Date completed: _____

Difficulty level: ◇ Beginner ◇ Intermediate ◇ Advanced

What I did with the finished piece:

◇ Kept it ◇ Gifted it ◇ Sold it ◇ Other

If gifted or sold, who was the recipient? _____

If sold, what was the price? _____

My overall rating of this product: ◇ ◇ ◇ ◇ ◇

Additional notes about this project: _____

_____

_____

_____

_____

_____

Next project planned: _____

_____

_____

Design name: _____

Dimensions: _____

Purchased kit from: _____

Price: _____

If the kit was a gift, who was it from? _____

Date started: _____

Date completed: _____

Difficulty level: ◇ Beginner ◇ Intermediate ◇ Advanced

What I did with the finished piece:

◇ Kept it ◇ Gifted it ◇ Sold it ◇ Other

If gifted or sold, who was the recipient? _____

If sold, what was the price? _____

My overall rating of this product: ◇ ◇ ◇ ◇ ◇

Additional notes about this project: _____

_____

_____

_____

_____

_____

Next project planned: _____

_____

_____

Design name: _____

Dimensions: _____

Purchased kit from: _____

Price: _____

If the kit was a gift, who was it from? _____

Date started: _____

Date completed: _____

Difficulty level: ◇ Beginner　◇ Intermediate　◇ Advanced

What I did with the finished piece:

◇ Kept it　◇ Gifted it　◇ Sold it　◇ Other

If gifted or sold, who was the recipient? _____

If sold, what was the price? _____

My overall rating of this product: ◇ ◇ ◇ ◇ ◇

Additional notes about this project: _____

_____

_____

_____

_____

_____

Next project planned: _____

_____

_____

Design name: _____

Dimensions: _____

Purchased kit from: _____

Price: _____

If the kit was a gift, who was it from? _____

Date started: _____

Date completed: _____

Difficulty level: ◇ Beginner   ◇ Intermediate   ◇ Advanced

What I did with the finished piece:

◇ Kept it   ◇ Gifted it   ◇ Sold it   ◇ Other

If gifted or sold, who was the recipient? _____

If sold, what was the price? _____

My overall rating of this product: ◇ ◇ ◇ ◇ ◇

Additional notes about this project: _____

_____

_____

_____

_____

_____

Next project planned: _____

_____

_____

Design name: _____

Dimensions: _____

Purchased kit from: _____

Price: _____

If the kit was a gift, who was it from? _____

Date started: _____

Date completed: _____

Difficulty level: ◇ Beginner　◇ Intermediate　◇ Advanced

What I did with the finished piece:

◇ Kept it　◇ Gifted it　◇ Sold it　◇ Other

If gifted or sold, who was the recipient? _____

If sold, what was the price? _____

My overall rating of this product: ◇ ◇ ◇ ◇ ◇

Additional notes about this project: _____

_____

_____

_____

_____

_____

Next project planned: _____

_____

_____

Design name: _____

Dimensions: _____

Purchased kit from: _____

Price: _____

If the kit was a gift, who was it from? _____

Date started: _____

Date completed: _____

Difficulty level: ◇ Beginner   ◇ Intermediate   ◇ Advanced

What I did with the finished piece:

◇ Kept it   ◇ Gifted it   ◇ Sold it   ◇ Other

If gifted or sold, who was the recipient? _____

If sold, what was the price? _____

My overall rating of this product: ◇ ◇ ◇ ◇ ◇

Additional notes about this project: _____

_____

_____

_____

_____

_____

Next project planned: _____

_____

_____

Design name: _____

Dimensions: _____

Purchased kit from: _____

Price: _____

If the kit was a gift, who was it from? _____

Date started: _____

Date completed: _____

Difficulty level: ◇ Beginner   ◇ Intermediate   ◇ Advanced

What I did with the finished piece:

◇ Kept it   ◇ Gifted it   ◇ Sold it   ◇ Other

If gifted or sold, who was the recipient? _____

If sold, what was the price? _____

My overall rating of this product: ◇ ◇ ◇ ◇ ◇

Additional notes about this project: _____

_____

_____

_____

_____

_____

Next project planned: _____

_____

_____

Design name: _____

Dimensions: _____

Purchased kit from: _____

Price: _____

If the kit was a gift, who was it from? _____

Date started: _____

Date completed: _____

Difficulty level: ◇ Beginner ◇ Intermediate ◇ Advanced

What I did with the finished piece:

◇ Kept it ◇ Gifted it ◇ Sold it ◇ Other

If gifted or sold, who was the recipient? _____

If sold, what was the price? _____

My overall rating of this product: ◇ ◇ ◇ ◇ ◇

Additional notes about this project: _____

_____

_____

_____

_____

_____

Next project planned: _____

_____

_____

Design name: _____

Dimensions: _____

Purchased kit from: _____

Price: _____

If the kit was a gift, who was it from? _____

Date started: _____

Date completed: _____

Difficulty level: ◇ Beginner   ◇ Intermediate   ◇ Advanced

What I did with the finished piece:

◇ Kept it   ◇ Gifted it   ◇ Sold it   ◇ Other

If gifted or sold, who was the recipient? _____

If sold, what was the price? _____

My overall rating of this product: ◇ ◇ ◇ ◇ ◇

Additional notes about this project: _____

_____

_____

_____

_____

_____

Next project planned: _____

_____

_____

Design name: _____

Dimensions: _____

Purchased kit from: _____

Price: _____

If the kit was a gift, who was it from? _____

Date started: _____

Date completed: _____

Difficulty level: ◇ Beginner   ◇ Intermediate   ◇ Advanced

What I did with the finished piece:

◇ Kept it   ◇ Gifted it   ◇ Sold it   ◇ Other

If gifted or sold, who was the recipient? _____

If sold, what was the price? _____

My overall rating of this product: ◇ ◇ ◇ ◇ ◇

Additional notes about this project: _____

_____

_____

_____

_____

_____

Next project planned: _____

_____

_____

Design name: _____

Dimensions: _____

Purchased kit from: _____

Price: _____

If the kit was a gift, who was it from? _____

Date started: _____

Date completed: _____

Difficulty level: ◇ Beginner ◇ Intermediate ◇ Advanced

What I did with the finished piece:

◇ Kept it ◇ Gifted it ◇ Sold it ◇ Other

If gifted or sold, who was the recipient? _____

If sold, what was the price? _____

My overall rating of this product: ◇ ◇ ◇ ◇ ◇

Additional notes about this project: _____

_____

_____

_____

_____

_____

Next project planned: _____

_____

_____

Design name: _____

Dimensions: _____

Purchased kit from: _____

Price: _____

If the kit was a gift, who was it from? _____

Date started: _____

Date completed: _____

Difficulty level: ◇ Beginner ◇ Intermediate ◇ Advanced

What I did with the finished piece:

◇ Kept it ◇ Gifted it ◇ Sold it ◇ Other

If gifted or sold, who was the recipient? _____

If sold, what was the price? _____

My overall rating of this product: ◇ ◇ ◇ ◇ ◇

Additional notes about this project: _____

_____

_____

_____

_____

_____

Next project planned: _____

_____

_____

Design name: _____

Dimensions: _____

Purchased kit from: _____

Price: _____

If the kit was a gift, who was it from? _____

Date started: _____

Date completed: _____

Difficulty level: ◇ Beginner   ◇ Intermediate   ◇ Advanced

What I did with the finished piece:

◇ Kept it   ◇ Gifted it   ◇ Sold it   ◇ Other

If gifted or sold, who was the recipient? _____

If sold, what was the price? _____

My overall rating of this product: ◇ ◇ ◇ ◇ ◇

Additional notes about this project: _____

_____

_____

_____

_____

_____

Next project planned: _____

_____

_____

Design name: _____

Dimensions: _____

Purchased kit from: _____

Price: _____

If the kit was a gift, who was it from? _____

Date started: _____

Date completed: _____

Difficulty level: ◇ Beginner   ◇ Intermediate   ◇ Advanced

What I did with the finished piece:

◇ Kept it   ◇ Gifted it   ◇ Sold it   ◇ Other

If gifted or sold, who was the recipient? _____

If sold, what was the price? _____

My overall rating of this product: ◇ ◇ ◇ ◇ ◇

Additional notes about this project: _____

_____

_____

_____

_____

_____

Next project planned: _____

_____

_____

Design name: _____

Dimensions: _____

Purchased kit from: _____

Price: _____

If the kit was a gift, who was it from? _____

Date started: _____

Date completed: _____

Difficulty level: ◇ Beginner   ◇ Intermediate   ◇ Advanced

What I did with the finished piece:

◇ Kept it   ◇ Gifted it   ◇ Sold it   ◇ Other

If gifted or sold, who was the recipient? _____

If sold, what was the price? _____

My overall rating of this product: ◇ ◇ ◇ ◇ ◇

Additional notes about this project: _____

_____

_____

_____

_____

_____

Next project planned: _____

_____

_____

Design name: _____

Dimensions: _____

Purchased kit from: _____

Price: _____

If the kit was a gift, who was it from? _____

Date started: _____

Date completed: _____

Difficulty level: ◇ Beginner ◇ Intermediate ◇ Advanced

What I did with the finished piece:

◇ Kept it   ◇ Gifted it   ◇ Sold it   ◇ Other

If gifted or sold, who was the recipient? _____

If sold, what was the price? _____

My overall rating of this product: ◇ ◇ ◇ ◇ ◇

Additional notes about this project: _____

_____

_____

_____

_____

_____

Next project planned: _____

_____

_____

Design name: _____

Dimensions: _____

Purchased kit from: _____

Price: _____

If the kit was a gift, who was it from? _____

Date started: _____

Date completed: _____

Difficulty level: ◇ Beginner   ◇ Intermediate   ◇ Advanced

What I did with the finished piece:

◇ Kept it   ◇ Gifted it   ◇ Sold it   ◇ Other

If gifted or sold, who was the recipient? _____

If sold, what was the price? _____

My overall rating of this product: ◇ ◇ ◇ ◇ ◇

Additional notes about this project: _____

_____

_____

_____

_____

_____

Next project planned: _____

_____

_____

Design name: _____

Dimensions: _____

Purchased kit from: _____

Price: _____

If the kit was a gift, who was it from? _____

Date started: _____

Date completed: _____

Difficulty level: ◇ Beginner   ◇ Intermediate   ◇ Advanced

What I did with the finished piece:

◇ Kept it   ◇ Gifted it   ◇ Sold it   ◇ Other

If gifted or sold, who was the recipient? _____

If sold, what was the price? _____

My overall rating of this product: ◇ ◇ ◇ ◇ ◇

Additional notes about this project: _____

_____

_____

_____

_____

_____

Next project planned: _____

_____

_____

Design name: _____

Dimensions: _____

Purchased kit from: _____

Price: _____

If the kit was a gift, who was it from? _____

Date started: _____

Date completed: _____

Difficulty level: ◇ Beginner   ◇ Intermediate   ◇ Advanced

What I did with the finished piece:

◇ Kept it   ◇ Gifted it   ◇ Sold it   ◇ Other

If gifted or sold, who was the recipient? _____

If sold, what was the price? _____

My overall rating of this product: ◇ ◇ ◇ ◇ ◇

Additional notes about this project: _____

_____

_____

_____

_____

_____

Next project planned: _____

_____

_____

Design name: _____

Dimensions: _____

Purchased kit from: _____

Price: _____

If the kit was a gift, who was it from? _____

Date started: _____

Date completed: _____

Difficulty level: ◇ Beginner ◇ Intermediate ◇ Advanced

What I did with the finished piece:

◇ Kept it   ◇ Gifted it   ◇ Sold it   ◇ Other

If gifted or sold, who was the recipient? _____

If sold, what was the price? _____

My overall rating of this product: ◇ ◇ ◇ ◇ ◇

Additional notes about this project: _____

_____

_____

_____

_____

_____

Next project planned: _____

_____

_____

Design name: _____

Dimensions: _____

Purchased kit from: _____

Price: _____

If the kit was a gift, who was it from? _____

Date started: _____

Date completed: _____

Difficulty level: ◇ Beginner ◇ Intermediate ◇ Advanced

What I did with the finished piece:

◇ Kept it ◇ Gifted it ◇ Sold it ◇ Other

If gifted or sold, who was the recipient? _____

If sold, what was the price? _____

My overall rating of this product: ◇ ◇ ◇ ◇ ◇

Additional notes about this project: _____

_____

_____

_____

_____

_____

Next project planned: _____

_____

_____

Design name: _____

Dimensions: _____

Purchased kit from: _____

Price: _____

If the kit was a gift, who was it from? _____

Date started: _____

Date completed: _____

Difficulty level: ◇ Beginner ◇ Intermediate ◇ Advanced

What I did with the finished piece:

◇ Kept it ◇ Gifted it ◇ Sold it ◇ Other

If gifted or sold, who was the recipient? _____

If sold, what was the price? _____

My overall rating of this product: ◇ ◇ ◇ ◇ ◇

Additional notes about this project: _____

_____

_____

_____

_____

_____

Next project planned: _____

_____

_____

Design name: _____

Dimensions: _____

Purchased kit from: _____

Price: _____

If the kit was a gift, who was it from? _____

Date started: _____

Date completed: _____

Difficulty level: ◇ Beginner   ◇ Intermediate   ◇ Advanced

What I did with the finished piece:

◇ Kept it   ◇ Gifted it   ◇ Sold it   ◇ Other

If gifted or sold, who was the recipient? _____

If sold, what was the price? _____

My overall rating of this product: ◇ ◇ ◇ ◇ ◇

Additional notes about this project: _____

_____

_____

_____

_____

_____

Next project planned: _____

_____

_____

Design name: _____

Dimensions: _____

Purchased kit from: _____

Price: _____

If the kit was a gift, who was it from? _____

Date started: _____

Date completed: _____

Difficulty level: ◇ Beginner ◇ Intermediate ◇ Advanced

What I did with the finished piece:

◇ Kept it ◇ Gifted it ◇ Sold it ◇ Other

If gifted or sold, who was the recipient? _____

If sold, what was the price? _____

My overall rating of this product: ◇ ◇ ◇ ◇ ◇

Additional notes about this project: _____

_____

_____

_____

_____

_____

Next project planned: _____

_____

_____

Design name: _____

Dimensions: _____

Purchased kit from: _____

Price: _____

If the kit was a gift, who was it from? _____

Date started: _____

Date completed: _____

Difficulty level: ◇ Beginner ◇ Intermediate ◇ Advanced

What I did with the finished piece:

◇ Kept it ◇ Gifted it ◇ Sold it ◇ Other

If gifted or sold, who was the recipient? _____

If sold, what was the price? _____

My overall rating of this product: ◇ ◇ ◇ ◇ ◇

Additional notes about this project: _____

_____

_____

_____

_____

_____

Next project planned: _____

_____

_____

Design name: _____

Dimensions: _____

Purchased kit from: _____

Price: _____

If the kit was a gift, who was it from? _____

Date started: _____

Date completed: _____

Difficulty level: ◇ Beginner ◇ Intermediate ◇ Advanced

What I did with the finished piece:

◇ Kept it ◇ Gifted it ◇ Sold it ◇ Other

If gifted or sold, who was the recipient? _____

If sold, what was the price? _____

My overall rating of this product: ◇ ◇ ◇ ◇ ◇

Additional notes about this project: _____

_____

_____

_____

_____

_____

Next project planned: _____

_____

_____

Design name: _____

Dimensions: _____

Purchased kit from: _____

Price: _____

If the kit was a gift, who was it from? _____

Date started: _____

Date completed: _____

Difficulty level: ◇ Beginner ◇ Intermediate ◇ Advanced

What I did with the finished piece:

◇ Kept it   ◇ Gifted it   ◇ Sold it   ◇ Other

If gifted or sold, who was the recipient? _____

If sold, what was the price? _____

My overall rating of this product: ◇ ◇ ◇ ◇ ◇

Additional notes about this project: _____

_____

_____

_____

_____

_____

Next project planned: _____

_____

_____

Design name: _____

Dimensions: _____

Purchased kit from: _____

Price: _____

If the kit was a gift, who was it from? _____

Date started: _____

Date completed: ___ _____

Difficulty level: ◇ Beginner ◇ Intermediate ◇ Advanced

What I did with the finished piece:

◇ Kept it ◇ Gifted it ◇ Sold it ◇ Other

If gifted or sold, who was the recipient? _____

If sold, what was the price? _____

My overall rating of this product: ◇ ◇ ◇ ◇ ◇

Additional notes about this project: _____

_____

_____

_____

_____

_____

Next project planned: _____

_____

_____

Design name: _____

Dimensions: _____

Purchased kit from: _____

Price: _____

If the kit was a gift, who was it from? _____

Date started: _____

Date completed: _____

Difficulty level: ◇ Beginner   ◇ Intermediate   ◇ Advanced

What I did with the finished piece:

◇ Kept it   ◇ Gifted it   ◇ Sold it   ◇ Other

If gifted or sold, who was the recipient? _____

If sold, what was the price? _____

My overall rating of this product: ◇ ◇ ◇ ◇ ◇

Additional notes about this project: _____

_____

_____

_____

_____

_____

Next project planned: _____

_____

_____

Design name: _____

Dimensions: _____

Purchased kit from: _____

Price: _____

If the kit was a gift, who was it from? _____

Date started: _____

Date completed: _____

Difficulty level: ◇ Beginner   ◇ Intermediate   ◇ Advanced

What I did with the finished piece:

◇ Kept it   ◇ Gifted it   ◇ Sold it   ◇ Other

If gifted or sold, who was the recipient? _____

If sold, what was the price? _____

My overall rating of this product: ◇ ◇ ◇ ◇ ◇

Additional notes about this project: _____

_____

_____

_____

_____

_____

Next project planned: _____

_____

_____

Design name: _____

Dimensions: _____

Purchased kit from: _____

Price: _____

If the kit was a gift, who was it from? _____

Date started: _____

Date completed: _____

Difficulty level: ◇ Beginner   ◇ Intermediate   ◇ Advanced

What I did with the finished piece:

◇ Kept it   ◇ Gifted it   ◇ Sold it   ◇ Other

If gifted or sold, who was the recipient? _____

If sold, what was the price? _____

My overall rating of this product: ◇ ◇ ◇ ◇ ◇

Additional notes about this project: _____

_____

_____

_____

_____

_____

Next project planned: _____

_____

_____

Design name: _____

Dimensions: _____

Purchased kit from: _____

Price: _____

If the kit was a gift, who was it from? _____

Date started: _____

Date completed: _____

Difficulty level: ◇ Beginner   ◇ Intermediate   ◇ Advanced

What I did with the finished piece:

◇ Kept it   ◇ Gifted it   ◇ Sold it   ◇ Other

If gifted or sold, who was the recipient? _____

If sold, what was the price? _____

My overall rating of this product: ◇ ◇ ◇ ◇ ◇

Additional notes about this project: _____

_____

_____

_____

_____

_____

Next project planned: _____

_____

_____

Design name: _____

Dimensions: _____

Purchased kit from: _____

Price: _____

If the kit was a gift, who was it from? _____

Date started: _____

Date completed: _____

Difficulty level: ◇ Beginner　◇ Intermediate　◇ Advanced

What I did with the finished piece:

◇ Kept it　◇ Gifted it　◇ Sold it　◇ Other

If gifted or sold, who was the recipient? _____

If sold, what was the price? _____

My overall rating of this product: ◇ ◇ ◇ ◇ ◇

Additional notes about this project: _____

_____

_____

_____

_____

_____

Next project planned: _____

_____

_____

Design name: _____

Dimensions: _____

Purchased kit from: _____

Price: _____

If the kit was a gift, who was it from? _____

Date started: _____

Date completed: _____

Difficulty level: ◇ Beginner ◇ Intermediate ◇ Advanced

What I did with the finished piece:

◇ Kept it ◇ Gifted it ◇ Sold it ◇ Other

If gifted or sold, who was the recipient? _____

It sold, what was the price? _____

My overall rating of this product: ◇ ◇ ◇ ◇ ◇

Additional notes about this project: _____

_____

_____

_____

_____

_____

Next project planned: _____

_____

_____

Design name: _____

Dimensions: _____

Purchased kit from: _____

Price: _____

If the kit was a gift, who was it from? _____

Date started: _____

Date completed: _____

Difficulty level: ◇ Beginner ◇ Intermediate ◇ Advanced

What I did with the finished piece:

◇ Kept it ◇ Gifted it ◇ Sold it ◇ Other

If gifted or sold, who was the recipient? _____

If sold, what was the price? _____

My overall rating of this product: ◇ ◇ ◇ ◇ ◇

Additional notes about this project: _____

_____

_____

_____

_____

_____

Next project planned: _____

_____

_____

Design name: _____

Dimensions: _____

Purchased kit from: _____

Price: _____

If the kit was a gift, who was it from? _____

Date started: _____

Date completed: _____

Difficulty level: ◇ Beginner   ◇ Intermediate   ◇ Advanced

What I did with the finished piece:

◇ Kept it   ◇ Gifted it   ◇ Sold it   ◇ Other

If gifted or sold, who was the recipient? _____

If sold, what was the price? _____

My overall rating of this product: ◇ ◇ ◇ ◇ ◇

Additional notes about this project: _____

_____

_____

_____

_____

_____

Next project planned: _____

_____

_____

Design name: _____

Dimensions: _____

Purchased kit from: _____

Price: _____

If the kit was a gift, who was it from? _____

Date started: _____

Date completed: _____

Difficulty level: ◇ Beginner ◇ Intermediate ◇ Advanced

What I did with the finished piece:

◇ Kept it ◇ Gifted it ◇ Sold it ◇ Other

If gifted or sold, who was the recipient? _____

If sold, what was the price? _____

My overall rating of this product: ◇ ◇ ◇ ◇ ◇

Additional notes about this project: _____

_____

_____

_____

_____

_____

Next project planned: _____

_____

_____

Design name: _____

Dimensions: _____

Purchased kit from: _____

Price: _____

If the kit was a gift, who was it from? _____

Date started: _____

Date completed: _____

Difficulty level: ◇ Beginner   ◇ Intermediate   ◇ Advanced

What I did with the finished piece:

◇ Kept it   ◇ Gifted it   ◇ Sold it   ◇ Other

If gifted or sold, who was the recipient? _____

If sold, what was the price? _____

My overall rating of this product: ◇ ◇ ◇ ◇ ◇

Additional notes about this project: _____

_____

_____

_____

_____

_____

Next project planned: _____

_____

_____

Design name: _____

Dimensions: _____

Purchased kit from: _____

Price: _____

If the kit was a gift, who was it from? _____

Date started: _____

Date completed: _____

Difficulty level: ◇ Beginner   ◇ Intermediate   ◇ Advanced

What I did with the finished piece:

◇ Kept it   ◇ Gifted it   ◇ Sold it   ◇ Other

If gifted or sold, who was the recipient? _____

If sold, what was the price? _____

My overall rating of this product: ◇ ◇ ◇ ◇ ◇

Additional notes about this project: _____

_____

_____

_____

_____

_____

Next project planned: _____

_____

_____

Design name: _____

Dimensions: _____

Purchased kit from: _____

Price: _____

If the kit was a gift, who was it from? _____

Date started: _____

Date completed: _____

Difficulty level: ◇ Beginner   ◇ Intermediate   ◇ Advanced

What I did with the finished piece:

◇ Kept it   ◇ Gifted it   ◇ Sold it   ◇ Other

If gifted or sold, who was the recipient? _____

If sold, what was the price? _____

My overall rating of this product: ◇ ◇ ◇ ◇ ◇

Additional notes about this project: _____

_____

_____

_____

_____

_____

Next project planned: _____

_____

_____

Design name: _____

Dimensions: _____

Purchased kit from: _____

Price: _____

If the kit was a gift, who was it from? _____

Date started: _____

Date completed: _____

Difficulty level: ◇ Beginner ◇ Intermediate ◇ Advanced

What I did with the finished piece:

◇ Kept it ◇ Gifted it ◇ Sold it ◇ Other

If gifted or sold, who was the recipient? _____

If sold, what was the price? _____

My overall rating of this product: ◇ ◇ ◇ ◇ ◇

Additional notes about this project: _____

_____

_____

_____

_____

_____

Next project planned: _____

_____

_____

Design name: _____

Dimensions: _____

Purchased kit from: _____

Price: _____

If the kit was a gift, who was it from? _____

Date started: _____

Date completed: _____

Difficulty level: ◇ Beginner   ◇ Intermediate   ◇ Advanced

What I did with the finished piece:

◇ Kept it   ◇ Gifted it   ◇ Sold it   ◇ Other

If gifted or sold, who was the recipient? _____

If sold, what was the price? _____

My overall rating of this product: ◇ ◇ ◇ ◇ ◇

Additional notes about this project: _____

_____

_____

_____

_____

_____

Next project planned: _____

_____

_____

Design name: _____

Dimensions: _____

Purchased kit from: _____

Price: _____

If the kit was a gift, who was it from? _____

Date started: _____

Date completed: _____

Difficulty level: ◇ Beginner ◇ Intermediate ◇ Advanced

What I did with the finished piece:

◇ Kept it ◇ Gifted it ◇ Sold it ◇ Other

If gifted or sold, who was the recipient? _____

If sold, what was the price? _____

My overall rating of this product: ◇ ◇ ◇ ◇ ◇

Additional notes about this project: _____

_____

_____

_____

_____

_____

Next project planned: _____

_____

_____